We Are Brighton!

We Are Brighton!

Two seasons. Two promotions. Two Championships.
Two unbelievable years in the life of Brighton & Hove Albion

©Bennett Dean, Paul Hazlewood and Simon Levenson

Bennett Dean, Paul Hazlewood and Simon Levenson have asserted their rights in accordance with the *Copyright, Designs and Patents Act 1988* to be identified as the authors of this work.

Published by:
Pitch Publishing (Brighton) Ltd
10 Beresford Court
Somerhill Road
Hove BN3 1RH
Email: info@pitchpublishing.co.uk
Web: www.pitchpublishing.co.uk

First published 2002.

A catalogue record for this book is available from the British Library.

ISBN 0-9542460-0-4

Picture credits:
All pictures by Bennett Dean, except for the following:

Paul Hazlewood: pages 6; 9; 36; 50 (top left); 66 (main); 67 (main); 100 (top right); 102; 105 (top right, bottom right); 106 (top right, bottom right); 114 (bottom right); 115 (top left, top right, centre); 125 (right); 130 (top); 138 (right); 142 (left); 151 (top left); 161 (top left, top right, bottom right); 162 (top). *John Elms:* page 5; 16; 17; 24; 26.

Editor: Jo Hathaway
Cover picture: Bennett Dean
Page design and layout: Pitch Publishing
Photographs by Bennett Dean (with Paul Hazlewood and John Elms)
Printing: East Sussex Press (Crowborough) 01892 654074

We Are Brighton!

**Two seasons. Two promotions. Two Championships.
Two unbelievable years in the life of
Brighton & Hove Albion**

Acknowledgements

This book would never have happened if it had not been for some keen and vital contributions, so we would like to thank: Paul Hayward for a fantastic Foreword; Andrew Heryet for swamping us with quotations from the players; John Elms for his guidance, photographic expertise and permission to use his images; Tim Colville for further celluloid assistance; Andrew Hawes and Ian Hart for their thrilling commentaries and great laughs; Roy Chuter and Paul Camillin for their support and quotes from the Albion's Seagull matchday magazines, and Derek Allan for the press passes. Praise and thanks are also due to Peter Naylor, James McCullough, John Hopkins, Paul Gilmour, Alan Budgen, Simon Cooper, James Nevell, Peter Thompson and Graeme Rolf.

There is someone who deserves special thanks and that's Jo Hathaway. Without all her pestering, cajoling and support we would probably still be talking about the book rather than doing it – you're such a star!

Finally, we want to thank the Albion for allowing us to live out our dreams and to a passionate, dedicated support, who are a different class. This book is for you.

Foreword

Brighton and Hove Albion are the club they couldn't hang, and here, captured in grin-inducing detail, are the unbreakable in pursuit of the unimaginable – a trophy, dammit: the first for 36 years.

First one, then another. Div 3 became Div 2, and the Albion were champions again, five years after the undertakers had measured them for a box. This is a book about joy and incredulity; about staring at the league table and suspecting it was an illusion.

The gallows humour of the late-Goldstone and Gillingham years gave way to the perma-smile of Withdean. Everyone beaming, nobody quite willing to believe. Payback for all that grief. Withdean may have made some clubs think they were playing a pre-season friendly in Norway, as Huddersfield's Lou Macari remarked, but few sides left Sussex suburbia with condescension still in their mouths.

Let's not get too biblical and say that the Albion were being rewarded for all that suffering. The club was revived by good people doing their jobs as God, or Dick Knight at any rate, intended. Bobby Zamora, that sleek and feline heir to Peter Ward, ran all the way from the Withdean Portakabins into the England U-21s. The glories never ceased. Two successive championships. Keep saying it. It will sink in. Like this book: pictures and thoughts from a dream that just got better and better.

Albion fan Paul Hayward
SPORTS WRITER OF THE YEAR 2002

"Just look at the last fourteen games of last season –
I feel the players, fans and management staff know
that we can do it. We won seven, drew seven out of
the last fourteen, and if you're going to do that in
the football league, you are going to get promoted…"
Albion player Kerry Mayo

"I look at a squad line up of Cartwright, Jones, Cullip, Crosby and Mayo, Brooker, Oatway, Carpenter and Hart, with Steele and Zamora upfront, and I tell you with pride, 'This will be our year, and these players will become a legendary side of the future under Micky's leadership', you mark my words…"
Albion fan Peter Thompson

"I remember the huge anticipation. I spent the morning on the hot, sunny seafront with several hundred Albion fans. The atmosphere was terrific, really buzzing. What a contrast by 5 o'clock: pure devastation."
Albion fan Peter Naylor

" I've got a thing about not losing the faith, and I am asking supporters not to lose theirs. We will get better."

Micky Adams

"The weather was skin-crackingly hot and we could feel the burning expectancy amongst the 3,500 Brighton fans packed into the away end at Roots Hall. I always stick my head out of the dressing room to watch the team warm up. It was no different today. All of a sudden the chant goes up of 'Bring on the Champions!' – we hadn't even kicked a ball. I felt embarrassed as I looked to my left at Alan Little, my Southend counterpart. He had this little wry smile on his face; he knew, just as I knew, that there were still 46 games to go – there are going to be lots of ups and downs – and I think he used it as a motivational thing against us. His team talk would have been made a thousand times easier by our supporters. You can't fault him for it, I would have done the self same thing. I can almost hear what he is sure to have been saying at quarter to three: 'Hey, have a look at these big time Charlies. They've come here with 3,500 fans in tow, more than we have got in our own ground. They're already talking about winning championships and going up, and they haven't even kicked off yet. Let's go out there, let's show them what we're made of, let's bring them down to earth!' "

Albion Manager Micky Adams

"There's an old adage that says 'success doesn't come to you, you go to it' – enough said."
Micky Adams's programme notes for the Rochdale match

"I know Bobby Zamora scored six goals in six games, but if you think about it, £100,000 is a load of money to pay for a reserve team player at a Division Two club [Bristol Rovers]. I mean, he'd only played about 10 League games, so that's £10,000 a game!"
Albion fan Rob Baker

"It was pretty obvious that I wanted to play first-team football, and at Bristol Rovers, Ian Holloway made it clear I wouldn't be getting much of a chance; Micky Adams said I may be getting a few games."
Albion player Bobby Zamora

"It don't think it will be very long before the Premiership scouts start coming to Withdean and the big clubs start bidding for Bobby Zamora."
Albion fan Tony Bernstein

"Some Albion fans bumped into former Chancellor of the Exchequer Norman 'Black Wednesday' Lamont on the disrupted trains to and from Lincoln. He was cathedral-hopping rather than ground-hopping, and some of those fans probably wished they had joined him as their team pounded the Lincoln goal throughout the match and came away with a 2–0 defeat."

Albion's Seagull matchday magazine

"I've never seen a game like that in my life. We had 85% of the game. We talked before the game about the fact that 75% of all the goals that Lincoln had scored in the last three seasons were from corners and long throws or free kicks and that we had to switch on and be mentally alert for those moments. It was a corner and a break from Cameron and their keeper had one of the best days he'll have in his career. We just couldn't score."

Albion Manager Micky Adams

"Why us? It is so bloody obvious that we are better than anyone else in this division. When is it going to be our time?!"

Albion fan Jon Vallance

"There was a lot of abuse. That was the worst I've ever heard it. There were a few people behind that dug out who were not very nice and there were more than a few calls for Corky and I to disappear. Calls for me to resign, I'm 'letting Brighton down'. It's a long walk off that pitch. It's a long walk to the dug out when you're not going well. It's an even longer walk when you've lost 2–0 and the boos are ringing in your ears. That was a low, low ebb. In my time in football I can't really think I've been lower than that.

You don't realise sometimes how the backroom staff keep the manager going and they kept me going that night."

Micky Adams after Kidderminster at home

"A lot of people fancy Brighton this season, so it was a good result and I don't think they'll lose particularly many at home, but I thought we were good value for our win. They had the majority of possession, but didn't do anything with it."
Kidderminster boss Jan Molby

"I don't know what happened – it was just a one-off."
Albion player Danny Cullip

"The players had a team meeting, and afterwards – encouraged by Micky Adams – they went on a morale-boosting team-building session. What was said behind closed doors I don't think we'll ever know, but I am sure that some of the more vocal characters in the Albion squad would have had their say, leaving others in little doubt about what they thought. Micky Adams was very keen on his squad being a close-knit bunch, and hindsight proved it was a theory that worked."
Albion Press Officer Paul Camillin

"It was a case of we had to iron out a few things and it got done – simple as that!"
**Albion player Charlie Oatway on the dressing-room meeting
after Albion had lost three of their first four matches**

"The Torquay match seemed not dissimilar to the O.J. Simpson trial – we had little or no defence, yet still came out with a bit of a landslide victory!"
Gulls Eye 2

"It was embarrassing – every time
I lit a fag, your lot scored a goal!"
Torquay United fan Dave Pick

"The scoreline flattered Torquay."
Brace-grabbing Nathan Jones

"Millwall was the turning point in our season. After the first few matches playing 4–4–2 when the results weren't the best for us, the gaffer changed the formation [to 4–5–1] for the Millwall away game. That gave me a bit more licence to get forward with Richard Carpenter and Charlie Oatway behind me – it was quite a fluid formation."
Albion Captain Paul Rogers

"Most fans made a head-down, hasty and noiseless exit from The New Den. Our cover was chillingly blown on the long, dark walk up to South Bermondsey station when someone's mobile phone suddenly rang out the chorus of *Sussex By The Sea*…"
Albion fan Alan Budgen

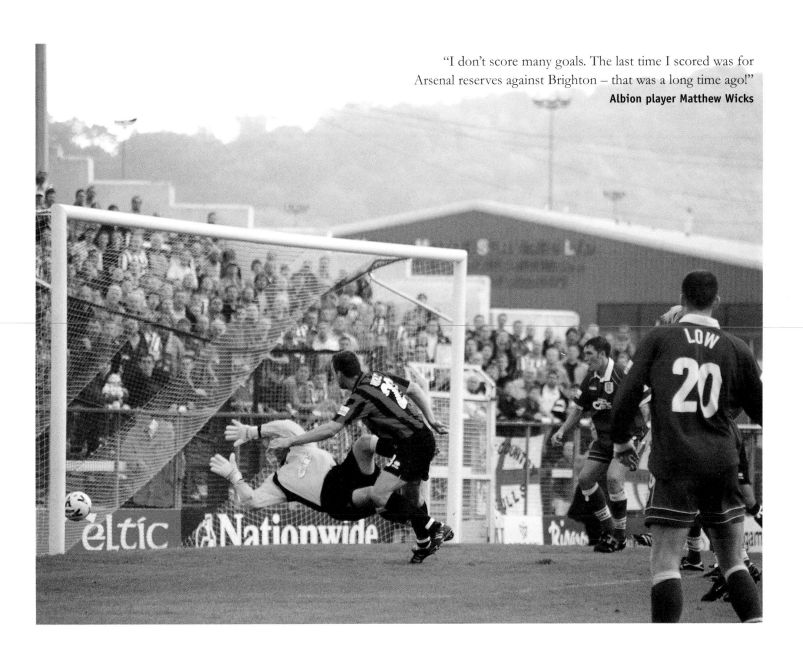

"I don't score many goals. The last time I scored was for Arsenal reserves against Brighton – that was a long time ago!"

Albion player Matthew Wicks

"It was 1–0. We were all over them. Then Bobby missed a sitter…

…moments later, City equalised."
Albion fan Jack Dunlop

"Perhaps if Bobby had scored it would have been a different result, but Cardiff are one of the best teams, if not the best, in the division, so it's a nice point for us. He is a very good young player with a very big future. You have to make little mistakes sometimes to get your knowledge of the game going again."
Albion Assistant Manager Alan Cork

"Protesters have blocked several fuel depots across the country, but a statement from the Government has reiterated that there is no need for panic buying." The newsreader sounded unconvinced. For "don't panic buy", read "PANIC BUY!". Three hundred and fifty Albion fanatics defied all odds and made it to Blackpool, dedication that proves how much our club means to us. And we made our presence heard – 350 sounded more like 3,500! Three hundred and fifty who weren't sure they were going to get home.

At half-time, their mascot paraded up and down in front of us with a petrol can…

We got back to Brighton in the early hours of that night in a car running on fumes, exhausted but with that feeling that what we'd achieved was something special."
Albion fan Graeme Rolf

"The thing that astonished me most at Blackpool was the level of support we had at the game, bearing in mind the current fuel crisis – you are all a credit to the club! We are more than flattered by your dedication to the cause."
Albion Manager Micky praises the fans

A HOME win over Torquay and creditable draws at Millwall and Cardiff meant the early-season stutter was banished to memory. The season was up and running, and as the team ran out to the applause of 341 hardy souls on a blustery night in Blackpool, they were about to embark on an impressive run of seven games without defeat that would thrust them into second place in the Third Division…

… AFTER A 2–0 win at Blackpool, the team went one better four days later at Withdean: a robust Cheltenham team were dispatched 3–0 in what turned out to be Alan Cork's last game as assistant manager to Micky Adams. He was on his way out of Brighton and off to join the Sam Hammam revolution at Cardiff…

"It doesn't come any better than this. I cannot recall – taking into account the strength of the opposition – a more complete home display since Adams took charge."

Andy Naylor writing in *The Argus* on the match against Cheltenham

"At the end of it, Adams purred 'We were awesome'. Thanks to a dozy copy writer, readers of the *Sunday Mirror* will have read it as 'we were awful' – anything but!"

Seagull matchday magazine picks up on some sloppy copy-taking at *The Mirror* HQ

"I was saddened to see him leave. I thought we were a very effective partnership, both here and at Fulham."
Albion Manager Micky Adams

"Corky was always good fun and his character goes much deeper than most fans realise. I will always have a lot of time for him. I could totally understand why he wanted to go – although he's never admitted it, I think he knew all along he was eventually going to be manager of Cardiff.

A few of the staff met him for a farewell drink in O'Neills Bar in Brighton – ironically, where it all began for the Albion – and at the end it was rather sad seeing him drive off for the last time."
Albion Press Officer Paul Camillin

"It was like leaving my brother to go to my father."
Alan Cork comments on going from Micky Adams to Sam Hammam

"Brighton are by far the best team
I've seen this season."
**Hartlepool boss Chris Turner after
his team lost 4–2 at Withdean**

"This was the Albion's fourth
season in the bottom division and
the present team was the best
I had seen in all that time. In the
previous three seasons all I ever
did was look at the bottom of the
table and calculate how many
points were needed to be safe
from the ignominy of the
Conference. Now the team were
at the top of the table and
beginning to purr. The buzz
amongst the Albion faithful
was deafening."
Albion fan Paul Hardy

…THE LOSS of Cork didn't hinder Adams or his team, as they won 1–0 at York and 2–0 over rivals Leyton Orient – enough to clinch Micky Adams his second Manager of the Month Award during his time at Brighton.

By the time Albion played their next match, at Hull City on Friday 6th October, Adams had appointed a new Number Two and coach – Bob Booker arrived from Brentford to replace Alan Cork, while Dean White made the shorter trip from Hastings to become the club's new reserve-team boss.

Hull also saw a return to action for Michel Kuipers. The Dutch goalkeeper had been subbed after just 45 minutes of his debut, but in his second match helped Albion to a 2–0 win with the first clean sheet of his career.

Kuipers followed that with a second shut-out on his home debut against Scunthorpe, but at the other end, Albion's forward arsenal fired a blank for the first time in eight matches.

With a trip to leaders Chesterfield looming large, an entertaining 4–2 home win over Hartlepool put Albion second in the table, setting up a first versus second top-of-the-table clash at Saltergate. More than 2,000 Brighton supporters set off up the M1 in anticipation…

"Who takes them is decided on the spur of the moment depending on where the ball is, on the distance and the angles involved. We practise a couple of times a week in training."

Albion player Richard Carpenter on taking free kicks

'Ryan Williams gets to the byline, chips the cross in – it's an inviting one towards the far post. Downward header from Jamie Ingledow and Chesterfield have snatched that late winner from the substitute just inside injury time. Brighton desperately close to holding out, but it was a low cross, they worked the extra man well. In came Ingledow late and his downward header beat Michel Kuipers at his near post. The sheer weight of pressure finally tells. Brighton all look distraught as they head back to the centre circle. It's Chesterfield 1, Brighton & Hove Albion 0.'

Andrew Hawes
BBC Southern Counties Radio

"This defeat will surely be more of a hiccup than a full-blown hangover."
The Observer, 22 October 2000

"It's worth remembering we may have lost a battle, but we haven't lost the war."
Albion Manager Micky Adams

THREE DAYS after the last minute defeat at Saltergate, Plymouth were the visitors at Withdean. The Albion had failed to beat them on four attempts the previous season; not a good omen, but the side took advantage of a poor Argyle side, with Richard Carpenter's crashing first-half strike, and a late goal from Bobby Zamora, securing a 2–0 win.

Saturday saw more than 500 Albion fans make the long trek to Darlington, where they were rewarded by another three points. Nathan Jones opened the scoring after just four minutes, and Lee Steele – on as first-half substitute for Charlie Oatway – netted his first goal of the season just after the hour, to put Albion in control. The home side did pull one back but Albion ended up worthy winners.

It needed stern words from Micky Adams at half time before Albion got going against the following week's visitors Carlisle. A poor first half had seen a Kerry Mayo own goal surrender the lead after Paul Watson's cross-cum-shot had put Albion in front.

Zamora restored Albion's lead within five minutes of the break, and a Paul Watson penalty, followed by Lee Steele's second goal in as many games made the game safe within 20 minutes of the restart. At times the team were less than impressive, but it's the mark of a good side that they can win 4–1 when not at their best.

A hard fought 0–0 draw at Macclesfield followed, and although Albion had a couple of chances to steal the game, it was a fair result, with the team putting on another durable defensive display, with Michel Kuipers in terrific form.

Ten points from the four games following that defeat at Chesterfield was an excellent response, and the team could look forward to the diversion of the FA Cup tie at Aldershot with confidence. In recent years, Albion's record against non-league sides hadn't exactly inspired confidence in supporters. But this team was starting to show its resilience, and despite the presence of the *Match of the Day* cameras hoping to capture an upset, even the fans were starting to talk of a Cup run…

"The best team we've played so far by a mile."
Jason Peake, Plymouth midfielder and former Albion midfielder describes the Brighton side

"The most exciting game I've seen in ages."
'Part-time' Albion and full-time Middlesbrough fan Mick Dunne after Darlington away

"I spent a lot of time talking to them about complacency."
Micky Adams, half time against Carlisle at home

"Certain pundits and cynics doubted us, and indeed [one journalist] writing in a non-league paper – stated that Aldershot were the best bet for a Cup upset on Saturday. Thanks! You certainly made my pre-match team talk and preparation a lot easier. I wonder sometimes whether these so-called 'experts' know what they're talking about."

Albion Manager Micky Adams

THE HOME match with Shrewsbury saw Albion pick up three points with another convincing win. The result was never in doubt after Gary Hart and Bobby Zamora gave Albion a 2–0 half-time cushion. Richard Carpenter added a third early in the second half, and Bobby's second goal of the game completed the rout.

A week later it was bottom-of-the-table Halifax's turn to test Albion's awesome record at Withdean, but it took over half an hour for the home team to turn their superiority into goals. And, boy, was it worth the wait as Bobby hammered home *that* goal following a mistimed clearance from former Albion full-back Chris Wilder. He added another in the second half, and the Shaymen's response was a case of too little, too late.

Cardiff provided the opposition in the first round of the LDV Vans trophy, and were beaten 2–0 thanks to early goals from Lee Johnson – his first and last goal for the club – and Danny Cullip. But the FA Cup trip to Scunthorpe proved to be a disappointment, with The Iron winning 2–1, and Bobby Zamora was sent off shortly before the end. The last Saturday fixture of the year also ended in defeat, with Albion going down 2–0 against Mansfield at Field Mill and giving one of their worst displays on the road all season.

But normal service was resumed the following Friday in a game notable for Exeter having ten players booked, without one receiving a red card. Goals from Rogers and Hart gave Albion the points to keep them up with the leaders. Boxing Day at Barnet saw the team keep up an unbeaten festive run going back to 1991 as they made light of the loss of Bobby Zamora through suspension, with Gary Hart notching a first-half winner in freezing conditions.

"He's got the same mental strength as Shearer at that age, and when I shout, he listens and doesn't let his head go down."
Albion Manager Micky Adams after *that* goal against Halifax

"Twelve o'clock kick-off at Barnet on Boxing Day – hungover on the coldest day of the season. I didn't want to be there; but then Gary Hart scores and I'm jumping up and down with 2,500 Albion fans because we're 1–0 up and we're going up."
Albion fan James McCullough

"Just a little word of warning for any supporters who are thinking of over-indulging during the festivities: take a look at Malcolm Stuart – that's what can happen!"
Micky Adams in his pre-Christmas programme notes

"Their football deserves a better stage."
Nick Szczepanik writing in *The Times*

"My game would definitely suffer if I tried to tone myself down. But it's nothing to do with being hard or soft, I'm just as game as anyone else and it's all about the side sticking together."
Albion player Charlie Oatway

Charlie Oatway was christened:

Anthony Philip David Terry Frank Donald Stanley Gerry Gordon Stephen James Oatway

after the 1973 QPR promotion-winning team.

"Nobody calls me Anthony, not even my mum. I'm called Charlie because of one of my aunts, who said that I looked like a right Charlie – and it's stuck ever since."

TORQUAY AWAY

"They were magnificent from start to finish."
Albion Manager Micky Adams after Torquay away

"Other than Chesterfield, Cardiff were the team I wanted to beat more than anybody else."

**Albion fan
Drew Carter**

"After Cardiff had tried to entice Bobby to south Wales with their £1.2 million bid – he's motivated by scoring goals, not money – it was great to see him get the winner when they came to Withdean."
Albion Press Officer Paul Camillin

"Micky Adams was a big factor in my coming here and promotion would be a fairytale – a fairytale I want to be part of."
Bobby Zamora, quoted in *The Guardian*

"I'd be a fool to want to leave Brighton."
Bobby Zamora, quoted in *Sport First*

"The way we're going I'd be silly to leave. I think we'd do all right in the Second Division next season. We can step up another division quite easily. I'd like to see out my contract at Brighton, but it's up to the gaffer and the Chairman."
Bobby Zamora, quoted on Sky Sports Website

"I don't want people to think, 'Micky bought this lad for £100,000, let's sell him and Micky will do the same again'."
Albion Manager Micky Adams, quoted in *The Guardian*

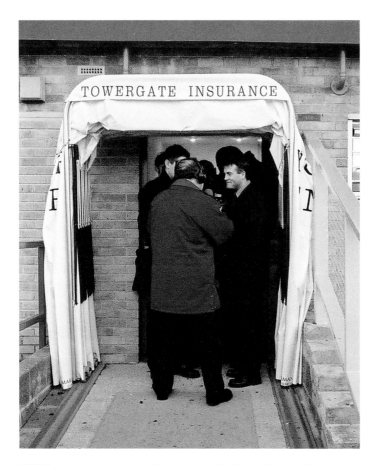

"Without wanting to make excuses for Saturday's defeat, our preparations were severely disrupted when the team coach suffered a blow-out en route to Whaddon Road…

To those of you that think preparation isn't that important, then I pose the question: why do we do it? We do it because failing to prepare is preparing to fail."
Albion Manager Micky Adams

BUOYED BY the home win over Cardiff, the squad were in confident mood as they travelled to Whaddon Road to face a Cheltenham side that had lost five games in row. Micky Adams reverted to a five-man defence, recalling Danny Cullip from suspension, but the day started as it was to continue, with the team coach suffering a puncture en route disrupting pre-match plans.

Albion's defence fell apart in the first ten minutes, conceding two sloppy goals. First, Grant McCann hammered the ball home from 30 yards, then Julian Alsop headed it in from a corner. To their credit, the team struck back immediately, with Danny Cullip heading home a trademark Paul Watson free-kick. Hopes of a recovery were given a further boost when the home side's Lee Howells was sent off after 20 minutes for a second bookable offence, following a clash with Paul Watson.

But former Albion keeper Steve Book was in fine form, making a string of saves as Albion searched desperately for a way through. But it was not to be, despite Micky Adams using all three of his substitutes, and when Bob Bloomer netted Cheltenham's third goal twenty minutes from time, the team had conceded three goals for the first time in the campaign. To add to Albion's woes, seven players found their way into the referee's note book, and Kerry Mayo would be suspended for the all-important trip to Leyton Orient in a fortnight's time.

A furious Micky Adams kept the players behind in the dressing room for over half an hour after the game as he read the riot act; Sunday's day off was cancelled with the players forced to report for extra training. Adams said of the performance, "They have been left in no uncertain terms what I expect. Up until this point the team has not let me down. But I am seeing signs now that when the going gets tough there are people not mentally strong enough and that worries me. I don't want us to blow it."

Matthew Wicks picked up a hamstring injury at Whaddon Road, but he wasn't the only casualty as Adams made changes for the visit of Blackpool. Nathan Jones replaced Wicks, Gary Hart came in for Darren Freeman, and, significantly as it turned out, Michel Kuipers returned in goal just three matches after being dropped for his poor kicking.

ALBION STRUGGLED to find any sort of rhythm in the first half against a Blackpool side themselves challenging for a place in the play-offs, with Andy Crosby having to make a series of fine tackles and interceptions. And it was Crosby who gave Albion the lead on 57 minutes. Watson's corner was headed goalwards by Paul Rogers, but Danny Shittu's clearance off the line hit Crosby on the ear and rebounded into the net. A stroke of luck, but one that Albion badly needed, as the home fans started to grow restless.

Blackpool continued to press for an equaliser, but the recalled Kuipers was equal to everything the Lancashire side threw at him, and in the dying moments he made the save of the season, somehow keeping out a close-range shot from on-loan substitute Richard Walker to give Albion all three points.

Struggling York City were up next, with another sell-out crowd anticipating a ninth home win in ten. It looked as if the team were on course to do just that when Gary Hart fired Albion into a second- half lead, but Steve Agnew levelled the scores for the Minstermen, and the team had to be content with a point, but still on track for promotion, despite slipping below Cardiff on goal difference following the Bluebirds 4–2 win at Kidderminster. But it wasn't enough for some sections of the south stand, and the team left the field to a crescendo of boos, prompting a furious reaction from Micky Adams.

"I was disappointed with them again. We didn't play well, but they are not helping. If you look at our Withdean record this year what have they got to moan about? I didn't tell them we have got a team that could rival Manchester United.

"They have got short memories. Two or three years ago we were in York's position. If they think we are going to walk our way to promotion without any help from them they are sadly mistaken. If they want to give anybody stick, give it to me and not the players, because it isn't helping them.

"I heard comments like 'spend some money', 'get a midfielder or a centre forward', but there *is* no more money. I am still trying to get two loan signings in but that's the lot. The fans need to get behind the players we've got."

With the crunch clash with Leyton Orient just a few days away, Andy Crosby urged the fans to get behind the team: "Three thousand fans for an away game is something new to me. It's a big game and the important thing is not to lose it so that Orient don't close the gap.

"The fans were obviously frustrated last Saturday, but not as much as the players. We all know we didn't play well, but we are third in the table. How the season finishes is in our own hands and we need their support."

Assistant manager Bob Booker, four times a promotion winner with Sheffield United and Brentford, said: "The positive thing to come out of last Saturday was that we didn't lose, even though it was frustrating for the players and fans. Obviously we were disappointed with a 1–1 draw, but we are trying to turn the negatives into positives.

"That made it four points out of six and if we carry on like that for the rest of the season we will go up. Every game is big from now on and it's all about picking up results, whether we draw or win. We ground out a result against Blackpool without playing the best and it's a case of continuing to grind them out."

To add to the tension amongst the 3,000-strong contingent of travelling fans, Cardiff beat Hull 2–0 at Ninian Park on Friday night to cement second spot in the table, three points clear of the Albion. Still, if results went right, a win over Barry Hearn's outfit could see Albion as many as eight points clear of fourth placed Hartlepool…

"We are Third Division footballers and
sometimes it doesn't work out right."
Albion player Charlie Oatway

"Would you leave the cinema five minutes before the end?"
Albion fan Chris Stratton

"How many of the 3,000 fans who exploded into song and celebration at the final whistle at Brisbane Road on Saturday booed the team off the Withdean pitch a week before? How many of the supporters who chanted 'Micky Adams's blue and white army!' were the supporters who had abused the Albion boss during and after the home game with York?"

Ian Hart, *The Argus*

LEYTON ORIENT AWAY

"'Albion in Dreamland' ran the headline in last Saturday's *Sports Argus*. Nobody who has been to Leyton would describe it as 'dreamland', but it was a great place to be after the superb 2–0 win against the local heroes."
Albion's Seagull matchday magazine

"We'll never play you again, again! We'll never play you again!"

Albion fans' chant at Brisbane Road

"You don't expect Bobby to miss from 12 yards."
Albion fan Brian White

"Zamora's tame penalty was more like a backpass for Paul Musselwhite."
Andy Naylor, *The Argus*

"He [Micky Adams] had every right to call us southern softies, even though I am not a southerner! We didn't work hard enough for him at Scunthorpe. I am just pleased we have bounced back. We were first to every ball and kept the tempo up. We have been in second for most of the season. We let it slip lately, but we are confident we can go up automatically."
Albion player Steve Melton after Hull City at home

"The more I work with him [Bobby Zamora] and see him play, the more I like him. You learn by your mistakes and he will get more goals this season. Bobby would be the first to say the result is more important than him getting on the scoresheet."
Albion player Phil Stant

HULL CITY AT HOME

HULL CITY AT HOME

"The supporters here are tremendous when the team is attacking… they make the difference between 0–0 and 1–0 and they have a big part to play in the promotion push."
Albion player Phil Stant

"We totally outplayed, outpassed and outworked them."
Albion Assistant Manager Bob Booker

As LUCK would have it, we found ourselves in the same hotel bar as Micky Adams, Bob Booker and staff the night before Albion's away match at Hartlepool. The team, with the exception of an injured Charlie Oatway, were already in their beds.

After being invited to join the group for a few drinks, and chatting about this and that, I asked Micky about the effects of the boo-boys; his face tightened. He told me that he'd never suffered anything like this at Fulham or anywhere else. He said he couldn't understand why, when we were flying high in the league, looking good for promotion, playing some good football and getting the results more often than not, fans were still complaining. I tried to explain my own theory on the matter.

"This club is just beginning to drag itself out of the darkest period in its 100 year history, and much of the credit is due to you and your team. The fans know that, it's indisputable. The problem is that now we can see things starting to happen, some are getting a little over excited, and sometimes that excitement turns to frustration."

Heads nodded, trying to understand, but still, neither Micky, nor anyone else could see how the history of this club could be blamed on either him or his players, feeling that, surely, the recent success was dragging the club away from all that. "How is the past our fault?" said one.

"Well, it isn't," I replied. "But if you'd been involved in the fight to save the Albion from going under, to the level that many of the fans did – one even went to prison – then you might understand why things are as they sometimes are."

The problem might be that we forgot the luxury of being 'run of the mill' football fans – those years took a heavy toll, taught us how to be desperate for our club on a day-to-day, week-to-week basis, turning us from football fans into political activists, now, apparently not always able to enjoy even our success!

Charlie Oatway offered a player's perspective:

"It's a siege mentality out there! Sometimes, it feels like everyone is against the gaffer and the players. We are expected to clap the supporters after every game, but sometimes you just don't feel like it, especially when they have been bombarding you with verbal abuse for 90 minutes."

I thought of how much I hate it when the players don't applaud us, particularly when we have travelled the length of the country to see them play, often spending a fortune along the way!

Everyone fights from their corner, I suppose. But it's important to remember, we're all meant to be on the same side!

* * *

Hartlepool provided possibly the strongest opposition we had encountered all season, but the boys showed their mettle and held out for a commendable score draw. At the end, as the players dutifully clapped the throng of Seagulls supporters in attendance, Bob Booker caught my eye at the back of the stand, and for the first time in more than 20 years, a personal clap was offered in my direction. It probably meant nothing to him, but it's something that I will treasure for years to come. It's funny how the little things – retaining the belief that manager, players and fans are all there for the same reason, and the courtesy to applaud that, even when things don't go your way – can end up meaning so much sometimes, wouldn't you agree?

Albion fan Paul Hazlewood

'Oh, Gary Hart, Gary, Gary, Gary Hart!'

FOLLOWING HIS 14-day touchline ban, Micky Adams was confined to a seat in the North Stand for the visit of Mansfield, and admitted to rather enjoying the experience. "It's always nice to see an overall picture of the game without getting too excited," he explained. "Managers rant and rave on the touchline when they might as well save their breath, because it's hot air a lot of the time." Adams was communicating with Bob Booker via his mobile phone, and caused much merriment when it rang to the tune of '*When The Saints Go Marching In*'.

The team travelled north to Rochdale looking for a first victory at Spotland since 1972, and they came within a whisker of getting three points after Richard Carpenter had given them the lead with a stunning free-kick three minutes from the end. But Lee Todd levelled the score with the last kick the game five minutes into stoppage time to salvage a point the home team scarcely deserved, much to the disappointment of the 522 travelling fans, another magnificent turnout.

There was more disappointment when Saturday's match with Halifax at The Shay was called off due to a waterlogged pitch. Astonishingly, televised Rugby League encounter was allowed to go ahead the night before, and it was obvious to anyone who watched the game that there was no chance that football could be played on the field the following day.

Lincoln provided the opposition the following Tuesday as Albion began the run-in knowing that they would be playing two fixtures a week until the end of the season. Phil Stant was on the bench against the club that had sacked him as manager just a few weeks before, and Lincoln included former Albion player Dave Cameron in their line-up. But the man dubbed the

'Weakest Imp' by one wag in the crowd was not to repeat his performance of the previous August – when he had scored against us – and Albion ran out comfortable 2–0 winners.

The result meant that Albion could seal promotion on Easter Saturday with victory at Home Park over Plymouth, but Hartlepool would have to lose at home to Hull and Rochdale would have to drop points at Macclesfield. Nevertheless 1,300 fans began their Easter holiday with a trip to the West Country,

wondering if this would be the day that Albion secured their first promotion in over a decade, but with a warning from Micky Adams to take nothing for granted.

"Plymouth is a very difficult place to go and play. I have not enjoyed too many happy times down there, but we are all looking forward to it. I am not worried about what Hartlepool or anyone else are doing. We are not there yet. We have still got to work for it. Plymouth won't roll over and die, as Lincoln didn't on Tuesday, so we have got to put our foot down on the pedal and go for it. I will maybe rotate the squad a little bit and see if some fresh legs can get another decent result."

"The atmosphere on Saturday, particularly in the last 10 minutes or so, has to be the best atmosphere at Withdean so far. Everyone seemed to be getting involved and realised that we had to lift the team in order that they held on to the 1–0 lead. And then Harty popped up with a great finish."

Albion fan Darren McKay after Mansfield at home

'There has been good news, bad news and even no news for supporters of Brighton and Hove Albion recently. The good is that automatic promotion is within sight, the bad concerns Bobby Zamora, their leading scorer, and there is still no news of a permanent home ground… Thirteen points from nine games before last night's match with Rochdale was the target for automatic promotion, the club's first elevation in status since 1988. Only Fulham can match Brighton's 15 home wins… To add to the feel-good factor, the club's supporters came second only to those of Leeds United as the most stylish in the country, according to a survey in *Match Of The Day* magazine…

'Now the bad news. Zamora, who scored his 25th goal of the season against Mansfield Town on Saturday, suffered a freak injury when a powerfully hit ball from Kerry Mayo, his team-mate, hit him and broke a finger. He was scheduled to miss the Rochdale match and Saturday's game with Halifax Town, after which it will be decided whether he will have an operation… That could rule him out for the rest of the season, but Adams said: "These things happen. We have got to get on with it and prove there is life without Bobby Zamora."

'Zamora has already repaid the investment of £100,000 that brought him from Bristol Rovers, who wisely insisted on a 30 per cent sell-on clause, last summer. Two seven-figure bids have already been turned down and, although Zamora, 20, admits to a desire to play at the top level, he has never indicated a wish to leave. Promotion could persuade him to stay a while longer…

'A problematic surface that makes Brighton's home record all the more remarkable, Withdean, a converted athletics venue, was never intended to stage league football and poor draining means that there has been difficulty coping with the 39 inches of rain that have fallen on it since September… Its 7,000 capacity is too small for the club's fan-base, whose potential is shown by recently published figures indicating that the average travelling support outstrips that of Southampton… Plans for a new ground are taking longer than expected to come to fruition. The club's favoured site, at Falmer, is situated between two universities and on the edge of downland, which will require delicate negotiations. [Martin] Perry, who was involved in the planning of the Alfred McAlpine Stadium in Huddersfield, hopes that supporters will be as patient as they are stylish.'

Nick Szczepanik, *The Times*

'Brighton and Hove Albion have today announced that their home match against Chesterfield, which was due to be played on March 24th 2001, will now take place on Tuesday 1st May, kick-off 7.45pm.'

Official Club statement, Wednesday 4th April 2001

"Looks like the Football League took our side and not 'Cheaterfield's'. Wouldn't it be nice to clinch the Championship at home against them?"

Albion fan Rob Bain writing on the Seagulls Mailing List

"Changing rooms are small, not comfortable. The pitch is narrow. Supporters are only on two sides of the pitch. There's a running track around it. Some refs allow you to use the multiple ball system and some don't, so it can be a bit stop, start."
Albion Manager Micky Adams talks about 'The' Withdean

"Lovin' it, lovin' it, lovin' it…"

'Melton into the mixer, the Frenchman Larrieu comes out, he's rather uncertain, bounces to Brooker, has a crack from the edge of the box and Paul Brooker scores! It could be the goal that takes Brighton into the Second Division. All the Plymouth players come across to protest, but the loose ball wasn't dealt with by the Argyle defence and Brooker with an outstanding shot thumping it in from the edge of the area. What a start! It looks like it's Plymouth 0, Brighton 1…

'Shot deflects in towards Zamora. Has he got the strength to hold the defender off? He has. Sixteen minutes gone – Plymouth 0, Brighton 2.'

Andrew Hawes,
BBC Southern Counties Radio

"If you can't play
for them, you can't
play for anyone."

**Albion player
Andy Crosby
praises the fans**

'It's goalless at Macclesfield! Part One of the equation is there. Brighton are surely going to win this 2–0. It's all up to Victoria Park now, where Hull lead by a goal to nil.

It's full time at Hull… it's full time at Hull. Brighton are almost there.

All we've got to do is wait for the referee to blow his whistle here! The Albion fans know that Hull have won. They know that Macclesfield have drawn with Rochdale. There was a huge cheer there. We've had the three minutes of injury time. The referee just has to blow his whistle to send Brighton and Hove Albion into the Second Division.

The free kick will be taken by Andy Crosby. According to my watch, it should be the last action of the match. Crosby plays it forward…

YEEEEES!… YESSS!… YES! [Ian Hart]

The referee blows his whistle and Brighton and Hove Albion are into the Second Division. After all the years of hurt… Now those fans away to my right, they have something to celebrate and the celebrations have started in that terrace. Absolute jubilation, a magnificent display at Plymouth Argyle to win Brighton and Hove Albion promotion. Brooker and Zamora tied it up inside the first 15 minutes, they were supremely professional, and so were Brighton. It was always a question of when, not if. It's here, at Plymouth Argyle on Easter Saturday that Brighton and Hove Albion have won promotion. Many many congratulations to Micky Adams and his side. A magnificent year!

What a great year, Hawesy. People laugh, they mock when you support Brighton, but this is worth it. This is worth all the heart ache.

Everything we've been through. The scum that tried to put us out of business, sold us up the river, where are they now?! Whatever stone they're under, we don't care…

The Albion are going up. Now for The Championship. Well done Hull, well done Macclesfield. [A Plymouth fan congratulates Ian by shaking his hand.] You've got to drive home now, mate! I'm sorry, it's just one of those things. It's going to be absolutely brilliant. We're going to get down to that dressing room, and we're going to savour every minute of this now.

The most glorious scenes… Brighton have the banner… The players all know… They're in front of the away end here at Home Park celebrating the moment. Television cameras in front of them… Micky Adams and Bob Booker holding up the sign that says they're promoted. Phil Stant applauding the Albion fans, Michelle Kuipers hugs his team mates… so many great stories in there. Richard Carpenter, now a four time promotion winner. Kerry Mayo, who was with the club in its very, very darkest days as a youngster, and who has come through. A Sussex boy, a Brighton fan, he's played his part in getting Brighton and Hove Albion out of football's basement and back, just a little closer, into the spotlight of this game.

Absolute delight away to my right. Bouncing up and down… blue and white shirts… flags waving… people standing, players at the terrace.

So many hugs, so many moments of delight. Individual, personal moments for those Brighton players, the first set of socks go into the crowd.

I'm not hugging you Hawesy, you can forget any thoughts of that! The players are punching the air…

Andrew Hawes and Ian Hart, BBC Southern Counties Radio

"The crowd are an important factor at Withdean. When they are good they are very very good!"
Albion player Adam Virgo

DARLINGTON AT HOME

'…a sea of delighted faces, open mouths and arms spread wide.'
Albion's Seagull matchday magazine

MACCLESFIELD AT HOME

"We're all professionals – we get paid to do a job
and we just go out there and do our job."
Albion player Bobby Zamora

MACCLESFIELD AT HOME

"One Micky Adams, there's only one Micky Adams…"
Albion fans' chant

"Micky is the catalyst that has transformed the Albion. It is said Dick Knight saved the Albion off the field, well there's definitely a case for saying Adams saved them *on* it. Without his ambition and foresight, I dread to think where this club would be."
Ian Hart, *The Argus*

CHESTERFIELD AT HOME

"May 1st, 2001 was certainly the most memorable Albion day to date in my life. Not only was it the last game of the season against Chesterfield but it was also my birthday. My mind wasn't on presents or cards but the making of a giant brown envelope in relation to The Cheats' financial irregularities during the course of the season. After several hours of hard toil in the garden, the mother of all envelopes was born. My baby measured 18 feet by 12 feet and was even adorned with a stamp and white label addressed to 'Chesterfield FC'. Within an hour of leaving home it had survived the car and park-and-ride trips and was passed over the fans in the South Stand. For me, it was as memorable as Cullip's match winner and the after-match trophy celebrations."

Albion fan James Nevell

'Goal kick forward, it gets trapped under Rogers's feet. He loses out to two players, and then gets in a vital tackle that wins it back, allows Mayo to stream forward, about 20 yards from goal. Mayo might go on, his own right-foot shot tipped behind. What a crowning glory that was for Mayo! Best one he's put in all season.

'Steele lines up right in front of the keeper, Pollitt. Watson drives in the corner – glancing header that might win the Championship for Brighton & Hove Albion. Drilled in by the Seagulls, they all run to embrace the man who scored! Everyone leaping around in complete and utter adulation! A magnificent header and Brighton are surely heading towards the title here at Withdean. Only 12 minutes left and it was powered in, it's Brighton & Hove Albion 1, Chesterfield 0, and I think the man to have done it was Danny Cullip.'

Andrew Hawes, BBC Southern Counties Radio

"Tuesday night and the taxi hadn't turned up. Too much time spent celebrating the Championship victory over Chesterfield had left me stranded at Withdean with little hope of getting back to Brighton station for the last London train of the evening.

Having already proved himself a hero with his epic winning goal that evening, Danny Cullip turned rescuer as he gave me a lift. I reached the station with seconds to spare, hollering, *'Hold that train!'*"

Albion fan Alan Budgen

CHESTERFIELD AT HOME

"He's a hardened professional doing a job and I am convinced it doesn't matter to Micky whether he's doing it in Brighton, Barnsley or Bridport."
Albion fan Tim Humphrey

"I don't think I'd realised how much success at Brighton meant to him until I saw him with that trophy."
Albion fan Darren Pannell

"It meant so much to me. I haven't seen the Albion win a trophy in 32 years. My sister had just died, and her kids were mascots at this match. When the winner went in so much s**t was released… the club had been through it and recovered – and so could I."
Albion fan Roy Chuter

SHREWSBURY AWAY

"In May 1997, two weeks after Hereford, I moved from Brighton to Wellington in New Zealand. Three years later, the Albion were on the verge of clinching promotion from Division 3 and I decided to return home for the last three games of the season.

My wife got to see her first ever game of football and I got to see Albion's first trophy during my lifetime. We nearly didn't get into the Chesterfield game. We were third in the queue when the final ticket was sold. But the stranger who bought the last tickets let us have one after hearing we'd flown in from New Zealand to see the game!

The emotional celebration after the Chesterfield game was fantastic, and I shook hands with several players – Matthew Wicks, Lee Steele, Richard Carpenter.

Days later, the Internet Seagulls assembled at the Prince Rupert hotel in Shrewsbury after the match: a forgettable game, a memorable atmosphere. Memories were swapped, tales were told and enduring friendships were made...

Thanks to the Internet Seagulls who have managed to make me feel closer to the club I love despite living about as far away as I can get!"

Albion fan Michael Wray, New Zealand

SHREWSBURY AWAY

'Brighton! Passion like fire,

Brighton! Bellotti's been shown the door.

Love you forever, give up on you never,

Support you for evermore,

Brighton!'

Krispies's *Brighton Eyes* song first sung

"I don't know who had the bright idea but it was astonishing to see, literally hundreds of fans form a guard of honour outside the gents at Warwick services after Dick Knight and Ray Bloom stopped to relieve themselves. The funny thing was that everyone knew they'd gone in, but of course you never know how long these things take, and each innocent person who came out before them was greeted with a groan. It must have been like coming through customs at Gatwick immediately before Oasis as an expectant crowd awaited their heroes.

The scenes as they emerged were reminiscent of the old North Stand at the Goldstone, as first Dick – complete with jacket and Albion shirt – and then Ray emerged, to be treated like conquering heroes. The expressions on the faces of the staff had to be seen to be believed. One old girl said, 'I've worked here for years and I've never seen anything like it'."

Albion fan Bill Swallow

"I've waited all my life to see Brighton win a trophy. My son's seen one before his first birthday!"
Albion fan Paul Taylor

"The atmosphere that day was incredible. I had goose-bumps for three solid hours!"
Albion fan Katie Heeley

"We are the Champions! We are the Champions!"

As THE Albion players sprinted from the pitch at The Dell on May 26th to avoid the hordes of souvenir-seeking Southampton fans, eager to claim their mementos of Dell history, they could reflect on a remarkable Championship-winning centenary season. The team had performed above all expectations in winning the Third Division Championship by ten clear points from their nearest rivals Cardiff City just under a month earlier, and they could now look forward to a well-earned six-week break.

But there were two clouds on the immediate horizon – the futures of the man who had masterminded that success, Micky Adams, and 31-goal hero Bobby Zamora. Since the departure of Glenn Hoddle from The Dell to his spiritual home at White Hart Lane, rumours of Adams's imminent departure to the club where he had enjoyed both success and popularity as a player were rife amongst the Albion faithful.

Despite the club issuing statements denying that there had been any approach for their manager, the rumours persisted, and two days after the Southampton game, skipper Paul Rogers issued a public plea for Adams to stay with the club.

"It's very important that he stays. He is the guy who brought all of the players in. He cleared the decks when he came and all the players who played a part this season are here because of him. Obviously we want him to stay, and the same goes for Bobby Zamora. We want them to stay from a selfish point of view, but if they get offers it is something they would have to consider when the time comes."

Two weeks later both Rogers and the fans were delighted, and decidedly relieved, with the news that Adams had signed a new three-year deal and committed his future to the club.

Adams said, "I am pleased to end the speculation, none of which has been my making. I have been very happy at this football club. There are things, which have needed sorting out and improving at the club, and the directors are working very hard on those.

"I have been moved by the response, especially of the fans, to the team's success last season and look forward to carrying that progress forward in Division Two."

And when Cardiff manager Alan Cork went public with claims that the Welsh side were about to offer Albion £2 million for Zamora, Adams reiterated the club's stance that the young sharpshooter was not for sale at any price saying, "It's not a case of selling Bobby. That situation is still the same: the boy is not for sale. I am under no pressure to sell him, I wouldn't want to sell him and we have had no new offers for him."

Of the squad that had started the season, Darren Carr, Rod Thomas, Mark Cartwright and the injury-plagued Lee Steele were all given free transfers, while Martin Thomas, with the deadline day signing from Swansea, found himself free to talk to other clubs and eventually joined Oxford United. Darren Freeman, another who had spent much of the season sidelined with injury, was offered a month-to-month contract in order to prove his fitness. Cartwright meanwhile, joined Steele's former club, Shrewsbury.

Kerry Mayo was rewarded for his heroics with a new three-year contract that will keep him at the club until the end of the 2003/04 season and, at the same time, the club granted him a well-earned testimonial.

Adams had made no secret of the fact that he wanted to bring in new faces to strengthen the squad, and to increase competition for places, and his first signing was Kingstonian and England semi-professional midfielder, Geoff Pitcher who took a substantial pay cut in order to re-establish himself in the Football League, after previous experience with Colchester, Millwall and Watford.

Former Fulham skipper Simon Morgan was the next to put pen to paper, signing a one-year deal. A versatile veteran of Fulham's meteoric rise to the Premiership, he had spent much of the past year out of action with serious knee problems. Morgan was delighted to be reunited with former team-mates from Fulham in Albion's ranks.

Another who had tasted success at Craven Cottage, Dirk Lehmann, a big, strong striker, and a force in the Keegan team that had won the Second Division Championship, was Adams's third signing of the summer from Scottish Premier league outfit, Hibernian. Adams was quick to stress that the German had been brought in to take some of the pressure off Bobby Zamora, rather than as a replacement.

The final arrival before the players returned for pre-season training was 30-year-old former Portsmouth right-back Robbie Pethick, from Bristol Rovers. Pethick had made nearly 200 appearances in six years for Albion's south-coast rivals, was a regular in the Bristol Rovers side that came close to reaching the Second Division play-offs in 2000, but made just 20 appearances in the side that was relegated to the Third Division.

The Worthington Cup draw gave Albion an interesting home tie against First Division Wimbledon, but with First Round ties now being settled over one leg instead of two, Micky Adams was adamant that his side had a better than even chance of success.

The eagerly awaited league fixtures followed two days later, with fans looking forward to visiting some new grounds after five seasons in the Third Division. The new campaign would start at the Abbey Stadium against Cambridge United, with promotion favourites Wigan the first visitors to Withdean for a Second Division fixture.

Off the field, the club responded robustly to the announcement from Brighton University that, after 18 months of negotiations, they would now not be supporting the club's move to Falmer.

Martin Perry, in an upbeat statement issued by the club, said that it had been impossible to close the gap between the University's and the club's valuation of the buildings that need to be demolished to make way for the Community Stadium. Instead, a planning application would be submitted to build the stadium just 200 yards away from the original site at Village Way South on land wholly owned by the Council.

Thus, on June 24th 2001, the club celebrated its 100th birthday in bullish mood, and with architects working feverishly to ensure that the much-delayed application was submitted before the start of the new season.

"I think we've got the squad to be challenging for promotion and if we all stick together, keep working hard and have a little bit of luck then there is a chance of it. I'm not saying we will, I'm not saying we won't, but we definitely do have a chance next season."

Albion player Nathan Jones

'Jones and Brooker linking great together. That's a lovely ball from Jones, Brooker's in behind the defence – pulls it back for Lee Steele who strikes the ball home into the corner of the net and Brighton's second-half pressure pays off... Lee Steele may well be coming off the transfer list now! He's the man in form in pre-season, now the man in form for the real thing. Eleven minutes to go – Brighton lead Wigan by two goals to one here at Withdean.'

Andrew Hawes,
BBC Southern Counties Radio

"If it were not for BBC Southern Counties Radio, my life would be less Albion than it could be, because my dear old Dad still sends me tapes of every game."
Albion fan John Wainwright, Australia

"We've got a good squad here and the gaffer's bolstered it with good quality players this summer. But we haven't done anything yet, we've just played a couple of games and got a couple of good results. So, yes, we're buzzing, but we're always buzzing – we were last season when we had a poor start. We knew we were good enough and strong enough to overcome that start and still go up – that's the nature of the squad we've got here and the team spirit."

Albion player Charlie Oatway

'It's Murphy against Michel Kuipers, Murphy strikes it — Kuipers saves, pulls it behind. Murphy hit it well low and hard, but superb work from the Dutchman to tip it behind, and it's a corner.'

Andrew Hawes, BBC Southern Counties Radio

"The supporters are quality. Brighton has got really super-quality supporters, because when you go away to hard teams you need supporters, and we've got a really great team of supporters, so when you've got that behind you, it helps a lot."

Albion player Michel Kuipers

"I think it's been a terrific first month; I think we can feel proud of our efforts – we've got a lot to look forward to. We never said that we were pretenders to the throne for the Second Division – all I've ever promised people is that we'd work hard and believe in ourselves and show the confidence that we are good players and I think that, so far this season, we've done that."

Albion Manager Micky Adams

"Our team digs in at the moment – we're good when the chips are down, and that's the sign of a good team."

Albion Assistant Manager Bob Booker

"I'd love to be here to see it. The way the board are talking about it, it will happen but we are talking a long way off. A manager can only look so far into the future, and my history suggests I'm not at clubs too long!"

Albion Manager Micky Adams

I was desperate for a good start as manager. I was leaving it more to Bob and Dean that day…
Bob picked the team and did the majority of the talking."

New Albion Manager Peter Taylor

"It's a buzz for the team – he's a great manager, you don't get to manage England without having ability in that respect and we're all hoping he can come down here and carry on the good work."
Albion player Bobby Zamora

'Oatway chips it forward, Rogers is onside, tries a glancing header, falls to Rogers in the six yard box. It's blocked – Rogers has a third go and Peter Taylor's new era starts with a goal from the Brighton captain that was all about persistence. Paul Rogers scoring after six and a half minutes. He had three chances to stick that away and he did so in an almighty scramble. What a start for the new man! Brighton 1, Oldham 0.'

Andrew Hawes, BBC Southern Counties Radio

OLDHAM AT HOME

'Six or seven would have been a fairer reflection from the chances created... Taylor's new players made his job look easy as they confirmed their promotion potential by tearing apart an Oldham side deemed to be close rivals before this game.'

The Observer

PETER TAYLOR'S first match in charge saw the visit of Oldham, led by former Albion player Andy Ritchie, and the new man had a dream start as the Latics were blown away by a breathtaking first-half display. It wasn't quite so easy the following Wednesday as Albion went 2–0 down to strugglers Notts County at Meadow Lane, but Taylor showed his tactical awareness, and goals from Hart and Zamora gave Albion a share of the points.

"I was delighted with the way the lads played," said Peter Taylor. "The way they started is the reason they won the match. They were very positive and played at a brilliant tempo. I watched them train for two days and did most of the talking before the game, but I think Bob and Martin deserve all the credit, and the players. I knew they were going to start like trains, because they are a very together group who give each other a gee-up at the right times. That is the beauty of them. You want to do well in your first game. The applause only lasts for two seconds if the performance isn't right, but thankfully the performance was excellent."

He also had lots of praise for Bobby Zamora saying, "Bobby is very clever. He has great awareness, and goals in him, as we all know."

Zamora's goal at Meadow Lane was the start of a run that would see him break yet another Albion record. The team won their next four league games by the only goal, and each time Zamora was the man on target. A disappointing draw at home to Peterborough was followed by a 1–1 draw at Swindon, with Zamora scoring again to make it seven goals in seven games, one short of the record.

December began with a trip to Bury, or at least it did for 845 fans. Who would believe that Bobby had scored a better goal than the one against Halifax the previous season? It was only when we got home and saw it on television that we realised just how good it was.

The Sky cameras were at Withdean for the FA Cup clash with Rushden & Diamonds, and Bobby duly broke the record with one of his less spectacular efforts. The Rushden goalkeeper prompted chants of "Are you Barthez in disguise?" as he made a complete hash of a clearance, allowing Bobby to head home from close range to make it nine goals in nine games, after a goalmouth scramble.

But that was to be the team's last win for over a month. The postponement of the home fixture with Reading was followed by a bad-tempered 2–2 draw with Chesterfield, Albion letting a two-goal lead slip through their fingers. More than 3,000 supporters saw Simon Royce – brought in on loan for the injured Michel Kuipers – perform admirably on his debut in the goalless draw on Boxing Day at Loftus Road. Another two-goal lead was thrown away three days later as Blackpool battled back to equalise in the dying seconds, minutes after Royce had saved a penalty.

Some fans were starting to worry that the wheels were coming off the promotion bandwagon as Wigan, led by Andy Liddell, put three past Albion without reply. Peter Taylor's tactics were being heavily criticised in some quarters, and even Bobby Zamora was starting to take some flak.

Taylor reassured supporters that the team would bounce back: "It was our fourth game out of five away and we've won one,

drawn two and lost one, which isn't drastic, but the players were very disappointed with the performance, apart from the first ten minutes. They've had a tremendous run and they should be proud of it. They will bounce back. It's very easy when you are winning every week. It's when you lose and the players get disappointed that you have to work a touch harder, but we will do that."

But the team got back to winning ways and Zamora silenced his critics in the best way possible with a hat-trick against Cambridge, although the team left it very late to beat the division's bottom side. The Chesterfield crowd certainly weren't silent as he scored the cheekiest goal of the season, flicking the ball away from the Spireites keeper and rolling it into an empty net to help Albion to a 2–1 victory at Saltergate.

P325 CEEFAX 1 325 Sat 10 Nov 19:05/32

BBC FOOTBALL

NATIONWIDE DIVISION TWO 3/4

Nov 10		P	W	D	L	F	A	Pts
1	Brighton	18	11	5	2	26	13	38
2	Brentford	17	11	4	2	35	16	37
3	Stoke	17	11	3	3	27	11	36
4	Reading	18	10	2	6	24	16	32
5	Wycombe	18	7	8	3	25	17	29
6	Huddersfield	18	8	4	6	27	20	28
7	Bristol C	18	8	4	6	25	18	28
8	Cardiff	17	7	6	4	26	20	27
9	Tranmere	18	7	5	6	30	26	26
10	Peterborough	18	8	2	8	27	24	26
11	Colchester	18	8	2	8	30	29	26
12	Blackpool	18	7	5	6	26	30	26

"I was a bit surprised at first. He's the sort of player who would die for the cause – 100% committed. I assume he must have fallen out with the management. Why would he want leave the club when we're top of the league?"

Albion fan Dan Tester on Danny Cullip's transfer request

"Danny is a very honest boy; he's been very upfront with all the boys, including myself. He's come out and said exactly what he is feeling to the Chairman and to the manager. The way he's playing at the moment, I'm very surprised that nobody has come in for him yet. He gave everything again last night for the club and he will keep doing that. It will be disappointing for all the lads if he does leave us, but we have to accept that it might happen and we have to make the most of him while he's here."

Albion player Simon Morgan

"Peter Taylor is slowly bringing his own ideas into the squad, which are good, positive ideas and all the lads are happy with that. I think that shows with the way that we play and the effort that we put in. It's all fitting in quite well and he's carried on brilliantly since Micky Adams left."

Albion player Kerry Mayo

"I think if you look at the goals that Bobby has scored then you will realise how important he is. But it's more than that. He's not just a goalscorer, he is a hard working centre-forward that helps us keep the ball and helps us get it back."

Peter Taylor on Bobby Zamora

'When the ball hits the net… that's Zamora!'

"We probably knew it was going to be a scrap and I think that's what it was."

Albion manager Peter Taylor

'Here's Watson, into Cullip, good strike, OOOOOHHHH good strike by the defender, who goes winging away in celebration of a sparkling goal… sweetly struck, left-footed… Danny Cullip is the happiest player on the field!'

Tony Gubba, BBC TV commentator

"We've now got two very important league matches coming up before Christmas and it would be lovely if we could maintain our position and head the table on Christmas Day. The big games keep on coming, and it keeps the season rolling on."
Albion player Simon Morgan

"Now I wasn't a Micky Adams fan at all – but he proved me wrong, whereas I'm a big Peter Taylor fan. I think he is the man for the job, but what with the way we are playing, unfortunately, he's proving me wrong as well!"
Albion fan Steve Ede

CAMBRIDGE AT HOME

"You don't need much motivation for Cardiff."
Albion Manager Peter Taylor

THE FIRST of successive Thursday night fixtures saw Brentford prove why they're one of the best outfits in the league; they steamrollered their way to a 4–0 win. Cardiff's visit was brought forward 48 hours due to fears of crowd trouble, and in the event the decision proved to be correct. For the second season in a row Zamora gave Albion the points. Another 1–0 home win, this time over Tranmere, was followed by a 2–0 defeat at much-improved Oldham. Still Albion were second, but they now faced their biggest test of the season: the visit of league leaders Reading.

Again, Peter Taylor backed his side to recover from a setback: "The players are fine. I told them the performance as far as I'm concerned was excellent. Okay we didn't score and lost 2–0, so that might surprise a lot of people, but the performance was fine. Reading are absolutely flying at the moment, but we intend to beat them."

Billed as the most important match of the campaign so far, the question was, would the game live up to expectations, would the team perform?

"The way Junior strolled onto Bobby's square pass across the six yard box and calmly side footed it in whilst in danger of being bulldozed by three Reading defenders summed it up – cool…"

Albion fan Graeme Rolf

"At the final whistle I was absolutely ecstatic. Not only at the result, but at the feeling that suddenly we have a 'squad', and the fear of fading away in the final months of the season due to injuries and suspensions to key players suddenly doesn't look so likely."

Albion fan Andy Heryet

"Brighton looked well organised and a fairly useful team. They are flying on confidence and are about to hit three successive home games against Northampton, Bury and Notts County – so that'll be nine points for them and they're going up."

Reading fan Mark Butcher

"We had to be at our best and I think… probably the most pleasing 90 minutes I've seen at Withdean."

Albion Manager Peter Taylor

'Hart to Carpenter, playing it to Zamora down by the byline. He's got some help there, gets it back from a little back heel… cuts in on his left and drives a superb shot into the corner of the net… A brilliant, clinical finish from Bobby Zamora on the hour mark! …and Brighton's dreams of the Championship are alive all of a sudden! It's Brighton 1, Reading 0.

'Zamora on the edge of the box, going for a little chipped ball… there's a great chance and there's a stunning finish to make it two goals to nil! I think it was Steve Melton who flicked that in, over the top… a little looping effort, looping over Ben Roberts and a stunning strike from Brighton. It's two in pretty much three minutes and the league leaders are heading to defeat here…

'Zamora's made a run through – can he apply the perfect finish? He takes it round Ben Roberts, he's been forced very wide. Zamora lays it back across the goal for Junior Lewis to score on his home debut with two minutes to go! It rounds off a magnificent night for Brighton! Paul Watson raises both his fists, punches the air! Lewis scores, it's Brighton 3, Reading 0, and the league leaders have been soundly beaten by the Seagulls now.'

Andrew Hawes
BBC Southern Counties Radio

"I think the atmosphere is great for evening games at Withdean and I always enjoy it. I think it is brilliant when you go down the tunnel in the dark and come out to the lights. I think the whole team like it."
Albion player Michel Kuipers

"If we get anything out of tonight's game it will be a miracle. So far, all the people I have spoken to have guessed at either 0–3 , 0–2 or 1–2 scorelines.

No-one seems very optimistic about this fixture; Reading are by far the best team in the division, and tonight is going to be the toughest test so far."

**Albion fan
Matthew Horrocks**

"Today held very mixed emotions for me. After five years buried in the lurid world of fanzine production, our current venture, *Gulls Eye 2* has ceased to be. At least it has been forced to fold at a time when the club is in a healthy state, both on and off the pitch, and the vital three points won against a promotion contender have opened up a little breathing space between us and the chasing pack. Hopefully, another fanzine will emerge to fill the void *Gulls Eye 2* has left, but in the meantime it is left to *Keep the Faith* to provide a voice piece for the fans."
Editor of *Gulls Eye 2* Paul Hazlewood

'Albion Chairman Dick Knight has launched a bid to buy out his predecessor Bill Archer. Mr Knight has been backed by current investors in the club, including DJ Norman Cook.'
***The Argus*, 22nd February 2002**

"Coming to The Withdean was like playing a pre-season
friendly in Norway."
Huddersfield Manager Lou Macari

"I couldn't get over how partisan the Brighton crowd were.
Every decision given our way was vehemently rejected
and the officials labelled 'cheats'!"
Huddersfield fan Bob Birkhead

'Brooker has it… puts a cross into that six yard box… and there's a goal from the late runner coming in from midfield! It's Brighton 1, Huddersfield 0… Margetson came for the cross and somehow never arrived and the Seagulls ended up driving the ball home. It's Brighton 1, Huddersfield… and I've got a feeling it was Junior Lewis again!'

Andrew Hawes, BBC Southern Counties Radio

"I'm almost starting to get excited now…"
**Albion fan
Russell Hedgecock**

"There are still plenty of shocks to come and we have got to make sure we are not one of them. We've had a brilliant season so far, we are in a tremendous position and it is up to us to keep going… I am still looking for 20 points. If we get that we give ourselves every chance."

Albion Manager Peter Taylor, quoted in *The Argus*

'Peter Taylor will quit Brighton at the end of the season, even if they are promoted to Division One. The former Leicester and England Under 21 boss, who turned down a five-year contract with the Football Association last season, is hoping for a permanent role in Sven Goran Eriksson's coaching staff after the World Cup.'

The Daily Mail

"...the most tedious two hours I have spent in ages... Still, at least we got a point!"
Albion fan Darren Pannell

"What a come down after the last couple of games. Memories of Division Three football came flooding back..."
Albion fan Brian White

"[Zamora had scored just before half-time.] I picked up the ball from Harty and had a good run. It was a bad first touch inside the penalty area and that took it away from goal. I had to cut it back from my left to my right and then I just hit it and it went in the bottom corner. In the first half we'd been a bit cagey. Although we'd scored the goal we weren't really playing as fluently as we can… They were putting in some dangerous crosses, and from set pieces they looked like they might snatch one. But once we scored the first goal [of the second half] it did settle the nerves a bit. Bobby's second goal showed what great feet he has. Junior set him up and the way he skipped past one defender and then rounded the keeper was very cool. As for Watto's final goal, I turned around to follow it in but decided not to bother because as soon as he hit it I knew it was going in the top corner."

Albion player Paul Brooker

"It comes to something when Brighton fans find themselves joining the Reading Exiles Supporters Club, just to secure a ticket for the game!"
Albion fan Chris Stratton

"The travelling support has been magnificent all season. I remember the Friday night game at Wrexham when over 500 travelled up – a brilliant turnout. We've only been beaten once away from home this season and we are very proud of that, and I think the fans are very proud too, which is why they turn up in such numbers. We want to see as many as possible on Saturday."
Albion player Simon Morgan

READING AWAY

READING AWAY

"Crap ground, crap weather, crap result."
Bury fan Jane Grigor

NOTTS COUNTY AT HOME

' Danny Stone… put in a wildly over-enthusiastic running challenge, forcing Bobby into an unplanned triple salcaud with double lutz and toe-loop as he flew through the air. Ice-skating judges would have marked it highly, but the tumble put his shoulder out.'
Albion Seagull matchday magazine

"When Bobby got taken off, someone from the club took me round to the First Aid room so that I would have the exclusive on his condition. I stopped short of actually going in the room – it was bad enough for Bobby that he'd been injured, the last thing he needed, lying on the couch in pain and uncertain of his immediate future, was to look up and see an Albion-loving undertaker!"
Ian Hart, BBC Southern Counties Radio

"It's the third time since I have been here that we have been 2–0 up and drawn 2–2. I am disappointed, because I thought we had learnt our lesson. We were unprofessional at times."
Albion Manager Peter Taylor

"If it stays like this (1–0 to the Albion) we can afford to lose a game, and that's assuming the other teams win all their remaining games, which they won't because they all have to play each other. I mean, how can we not go up?"
Albion fan Gavin Crute, half-time against Notts County at home

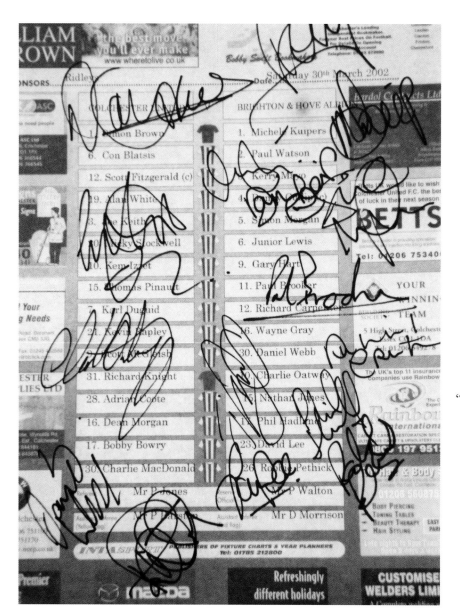

"I know what I can do. I scored six goals in fifteen starts on loan to Leyton Orient and I really enjoyed being involved in the first team. Brighton have given me an opportunity as well and hopefully I can grasp it with both hands. If I get enough chances and we play well as a team I have a lot of confidence in myself that I will score goals. Bobby's been terrific and he's had a great season for Brighton. Now I would like to score and help them get into Division One."

Albion player Wayne Gray on loan from Wimbledon, before his debut at Colchester

'Hart striding forward, Brighton have men in numbers here, Hart going through on the right hand side, laid off to Brooker, on the edge of the six yard box, Brooker tries to just flick it in there and it's gone in, it might have taken a deflection on the way but Paul Brooker makes it three inside ten minutes and this is turning into a sensational Brighton Performance now. Hart won the ball on the right hand side carried on into the penalty area, he fed Brooker, broke further to the byline, just flicked it back across the goal and in it went. It's 3–0 to the Seagulls. Extraordinary stuff.'

Andrew Hawes, BBC Southern Counties Radio

BRISTOL CITY AT HOME

"Brighton 1, Bristol City 1 – it's been hard work. Hart with the ball in diving header – goal! Brighton have done it right at the end, thanks to Lee Steele. Unbelievable stuff from the Seagulls in injury time! Quite amazing! City almost score, Brighton go down the end, Steele's unmarked, glanced it into the corner. It's 2–1 to the Seagulls. They're top of the table – Reading and Brentford, you've got a match here!"
Andrew Hawes,
BBC Southern Counties Radio

"I went for a jog last night and said to myself that I didn't care if we played the worst we have played for a million years, so long as we won."
Albion Manager Peter Taylor

"We dominated the game but could not finish them off –
their keeper was magnificent."
Bristol City Manager and former Albion player Danny Wilson

"We're all in this together – players and fans. The Brighton supporters have done tremendously well to help the club get to where they are now. They have got high expectations and possibly the last three or four home performances haven't lived up to those expectations. We're still very confident in the dressing room, and we know we'll have their full backing on Saturday. There is sure to be a large following there and hopefully, they will cheer us on to victory."
Albion player Simon Morgan

"Brighton has got great support and I expect 4,000 Seagulls fans to get behind the team to enable them to win their last few games."

Peterborough Manager Barry Fry

"I don't always tell the 100 per cent truth. Bobby is that important to us that it was worth taking the risk. To be fair to our physio Malcolm Stuart, he thought he had a chance of being fit for Peterborough the Monday after he did the injury."

Albion Manager Peter Taylor

"Peter has worked miracles in a short period of time at Brighton and all the fans are very excited with the prospect of getting two promotions in successive seasons. Brighton are a very hard team to beat and they have the least number of defeats this season because Peter has them well organised, with excellent discipline – they keep their shape and are deadly on set pieces."
Peterborough Manager Barry Fry

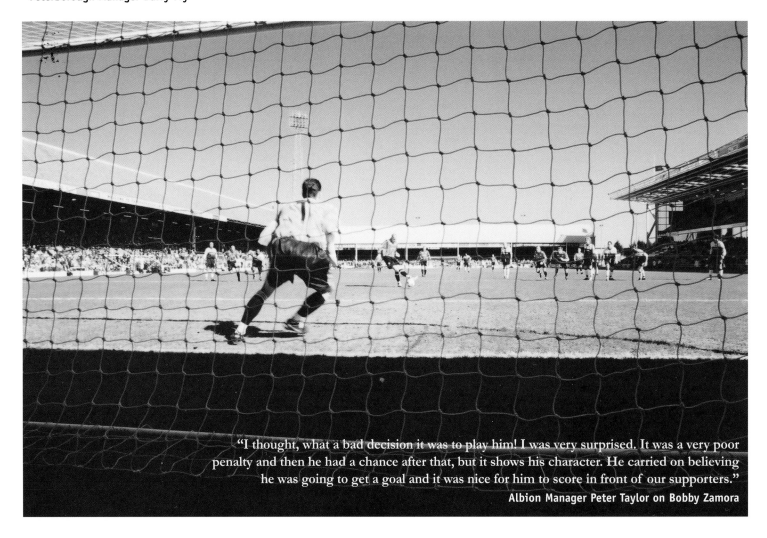

"I thought, what a bad decision it was to play him! I was very surprised. It was a very poor penalty and then he had a chance after that, but it shows his character. He carried on believing he was going to get a goal and it was nice for him to score in front of our supporters."
Albion Manager Peter Taylor on Bobby Zamora

"I understood he was still injured. At half-time I thought our luck was in… but then he scored."

Peterborough Manager Barry Fry

"There was a strange subdued promotion celebration the next day when Reading blew two more points. We were hacking down the A12 at the time, then it took an age to get through London and all we wanted was to do was get home and be with people who felt the same way as we did…. When we got back to Brighton, we all piled into the Evening Star, delirious and thirsty. There was a blues guitarist playing that night; one half of the pub was singing Albion songs, laughing and bouncing around, the other was nodding along to 'My woman done left me, look at the tears fall'. Weird but great!"

Albion fan Roy Chuter

'Peter Taylor admitted he could not bear to watch Brighton get promoted. The Seagulls boss knew if Reading failed to win at Tranmere yesterday then his boys were up. But Taylor bottled out watching the scores flick up on Teletext as a topsy-turvy tussle at Prenton Park finished 2–2. The former England chief admitted: "It was horrible following it this way, particularly when Reading pulled back. In the end I had to switch off and try and watch the Leeds-Sunderland match on TV instead."'

The Sun

'Knight has been the driving force.'
Andrew Dillon in *The Sun*

"I know a lot of fans would not be here if the Albion were not top of the league but when you have people climbing trees just to get a view of the game, something must be done about getting a new ground."

Albion fan Brian White on the 'Treegulls' phenomenon

"I only have to see the trophy in the hands of a Brighton captain to know that all the hard work has been worth it."
Albion Chairman Dick Knight

"There have been a lot of people knocking us and the ground and not giving us the credit we have deserved. The teams up there with us have been naming the best sides and not even putting us in the picture, which is a bit shameful considering what we have achieved with limited resources. I've never known a league table to lie. When you get relegated you deserve it and when you go up you deserve it, it is as simple as that."
Albion player Charlie Oatway

SWINDON AT HOME

"This is fantastic. Everything is going extremely well. We have got the team, we have got the supporters and all we need now is a new ground."
Martin Perry after Swindon

"This is a marvellous day. It is the players who deserve all the credit. We are going to do everything we can to keep the squad together and to strengthen it."
Dick Knight after Swindon

"I am lost for words. The last few minutes have been unbearable. I am shaking!"

"The first division is going to be about survival and will be very tough but it feels brilliant."
Norman Cook after Swindon

"It was a bit strange to find out while sitting in the garden, but it's a fantastic achievement. At the start of the season, realistically we thought about mid-table and pushing for the play-offs, but we have continued on a roll. If we win on Saturday we win the Championship and that's the next target. Nobody will be relaxing."

Albion Captain Paul Rogers on finding out Albion had been promoted

"The whole town went wild that evening. Forget the match – remember the experience."

Albion fan Pete Thompson

PORT VALE AWAY

Poetry in Promotion

The Guardian may not agree.
My critics will no-no it.
But now I am officially
a First Division Poet!

Five years ago this hapless bard
was in Division Three:
The Part Time Poets' Conference
Loomed large and ominously…

My home was sold beneath my feet
by men of foul intent:
Two years I penned my verses in
an outside bog in Kent.

But now I'm in a council place
Back in my old location
And though it's nowhere big enough
I'm filled with inspiration!

My poetry got better:
verbs and nouns began to gel
Last year I got promotion –
and a Championship as well!

At ten to five last Sunday
In a pub near Basildon
I stood on stage and yelled with pride
"I'm in Division One!"

A First Division Poet
In Residence, that's me –
At First Division Brighton
And Hove Albion FC!

It's five years since the Goldstone died.
Five years from then to now.
You want a rollercoaster?
You've got one, folks – and how!

It's onwards now and upwards
So, Council, listen here!
We need a proper stadium.
Now get your arse in gear!

Well done to Peter and the boys,
To Dick and Martin too.
We've seen it all, through thick and thin.
It's like a dream come true.

**Attila the Stockbroker aka John Baine, inspired by Dick Knight's
question: "How does it feel to be a First Division Poet in Residence?"**

"It's very emotional. I can't help shedding a tear at how far we have come in such a short time. So many people came out who cannot get in to watch us at Withdean. The enormous following we have puts out a very clear message that this is a unique club with a unique role in the community. That is why we need a stadium."

Albion Chairman Dick Knight

"This is how much the Albion means to Brighton and Hove. We all know football is a community thing. It is a dream we can all share together. If you're young you'll remember this day as long as you live. If you are older you'll appreciate it as we have been waiting for it for a long time. The team did it because they had more class, more team spirit and more absolute determination than the rest of the league put together."

**Albion Chairman
Dick Knight**

"It means everything to everyone here... because of where we've been in the past – what a wonderful day."
Albion Chairman Dick Knight

Epilogue

The door on the trophy cabinet had barely clicked shut when Peter Taylor called time on his Albion career. He walked away, citing his main reason as a lack of funds for the survival fight ahead in Division One.

We'd all spent the season getting used to the rockets exploding around Withdean, but not many of us expected this Catherine Wheel to start spinning so soon; the World Cup was supposed to provide the summer fireworks before the sky above Brighton lit up again.

Managers have walked away before and the Albion are by now well used to losing good men. "We've grown stronger for it," mused Dick Knight – a man who, with the future of English football in the balance, quite rightly wouldn't put the club in hock. Not even to keep one of the country's most highly-regarded coaches on the payroll.

As I write, Dick Knight is still auditioning for lead roles in the next episode of the Albion story, with loyalty pretty high up on his checklist. Bob Booker – a man who depicts the dictionary definition of loyalty, and who is surely a lead role in the making – has pledged his future to the club because he wants to be in Brighton for the day Division One rolls into town.

Whoever Dick Knight eventually chooses, we should feel content with his judgement; his track record on decision-making is as sparkling as those two trophies he held aloft at the end of the season.

The decision taken by Brighton & Hove City Council on June 12th is even more important than this. Blind to the outcome, I can only hope that the Council's Planning Committee has made the right one, and that a stadium matching the club's standing and future ambitions is now another step closer.

Whatever their decision, we are Brighton and will always be Brighton.

Albion fan Paul Camillin
Press Officer, Brighton & Hove Albion

2000/2001 Season

Date/fixture	Team played	Score (BHA–)	BHA goal scorers	Date/fixture	Team played	Score (BHA–)	BHA goal scorers
12 August	Southend (a)	0–2		22 December	Exeter (h)	2–0	Rogers 19; Hart 61
19 August	Rochdale (h)	2–1	Zamora 18, 45	26 December	Barnet (a)	1–0	Hart 31
22 August	League Cup v Millwall (h)	1–2	Watson 44	1 January 2001	Southend (h)	0–2	
26 August	Lincoln (a)	0–2		9 January	LDV Vans v Brentford (h)	2–2	*(Brentford win penalty shoot out)*
28 August	Kidderminster (h)	0–2			*Played at Griffin Park as Withdean unfit*		Brooker 24; Zamora 27
2 September	Torquay (h)	6–2	Zamora 10, 64, 85; Hart 20; Jones 30, 45	13 January	Kidderminster (a)	2–0	OG 37; Zamora 78
5 September	League Cup v Millwall (a)	1–1	Jones 67	27 January	Exeter (a)	0–1	
9 September	Cardiff (a)	1–1	Wicks 59	3 February	Torquay (a)	1–0	Zamora 75
12 September	Blackpool (a)	2–0	Rogers 33; Hart 45	10 February	Cardiff (h)	1–0	Zamora 15
16 September	Cheltenham (h)	3–0	Wicks 58; Watson 74 (pen); Zamora 88	17 February	Cheltenham (a)	1–3	Cullip 14
23 September	York (a)	1–0	Jones 35	20 February	Blackpool (h)	1–0	Crosby 57
30 September	Leyton Orient (h)	2–0	Rogers 42; Mayo 65	24 February	York (h)	1–1	Hart 55
6 October	Hull City (a)	2–0	Wicks 65; Rogers 74	3 March	Leyton Orient (a)	2–0	Brooker 29; Zamora 46
14 October	Scunthorpe (h)	0–0		6 March	Scunthorpe (a)	1–2	Brooker 4
18 October	Hartlepool (h)	4–2	Hart 7; Zamora 22, 68; Carpenter 30	10 March	Hull City (h)	3–0	Watson 42; Melton 69; Stant 88
21 October	Chesterfield (a)	0–1		14 March	Barnet (h)	4–1	Crosby 36; Zamora 37, 62; Rogers 54
24 October	Plymouth (h)	2–0	Carpenter 37; Zamora 85	17 March	Hartlepool (a)	2–2	Carpenter 37; Zamora 56 (pen)
28 October	Darlington (a)	2–1	Jones 4; Steele 63	31 March	Mansfield (h)	2–0	Zamora 18; Hart 90
4 November	Carlisle (h)	4–1	Watson 21, 62 (pen); Zamora 49; Steele 65	3 April	Rochdale (a)	1–1	Carpenter 87
11 November	Macclesfield (a)	0–0		10 April	Lincoln (h)	2–0	Rogers 34; Zamora 67
18 November	FA Cup v Aldershot (a)	6–2	Carpenter 2; Watson 43 (pen), 60 (pen); Oatway 53; Zamora 75; Wicks 77	14 April	Plymouth (a)	2–0	Brooker 3; Zamora 16
25 November	Shrewsbury (h)	4–0	Hart 7; Zamora 36, 82; Carpenter 55	16 April	Darlington (h)	2–0	Carpenter 28; Zamora 29
2 December	Halifax (h)	2–1	Zamora 35, 52	21 April	Carlisle (a)	0–0	
9 December	LDV Vans v Cardiff (h)	2–0	Johnson 13; Cullip 20	28 April	Macclesfield (h)	4–1	Zamora 20, 34 (pen), 80; Watson 87
9 December	FA Cup v Scunthorpe (a)	1–2	Zamora 15	1 May	Chesterfield (h)	1–0	Cullip 78
16 December	Mansfield (a)	0–2		3 May	Halifax (a)	0–0	
				5 May	Shrewsbury (a)	0–3	

2001/2002 Season

Date/fixture	Team played	Score (BHA–)	BHA goal scorers	Date/fixture	Team played	Score (BHA–)	BHA goal scorers
11 August	Cambridge (a)	0–0		8 December	FA Cup v Rushden & Diamonds	2–1	Zamora 6; Cullip 51
18 August	Wigan (h)	2–1	Zamora (pen) 39; Steele 79	21 December	Chesterfield (h)	2–2	Zamora 5; Steele 49
21 August	Worthington Cup v Wimbledon (h)	2–1	Zamora 57, 65	26 December	Queens Park Rangers (a)	0–0	
25 August	Tranmere (a)	0–0		29 December	Blackpool (a)	2–2	Steele 20; Jones 39
27 August	Blackpool (h)	4–0	Oatway 38; Carpenter 47; Steele 62; Zamora 72	12 January 2002	Wigan (a)	0–3	
				15 January	FA Cup v Preston (h)	0–2	
31 August	Northampton (a)	0–2		19 January	Cambridge (h)	4–3	Hart 25; Zamora 50 (pen), 75, 89
8 September	Queens Park Rangers (h)	2–1	Zamora 66; Watson 90	21 January	Chesterfield (a)	2–1	Zamora 49, 68
11 September	Worthington Cup v Southampton (h)	0–3		24 January	Brentford (a)	0–4	
14 September	Wrexham (a)	2–1	Zamora 68, 76 (pen)	31 January	Cardiff (h)	1–0	Zamora 14 (pen)
18 September	Stoke (h)	1–0	Watson 90	5 February	Tranmere (h)	1–0	Hart 61
22 September	Bournemouth (h)	2–1	Watson 13; OG 80	9 February	Oldham (a)	0–2	
25 September	Wycombe (a)	1–1	Jones 11	11 February	Reading (h)	3–1	Zamora 60; Melton 64; Lewis 88
29 September	Cardiff (a)	1–1	Zamora 36	16 February	Huddersfield (h)	1–0	Lewis 54
5 October	Brentford (h)	1–2	Steele 52	23 February	Wrexham (h)	0–0	
13 October	Huddersfield (a)	2–1	Zamora 35; Hart 64	26 February	Bournemouth (a)	1–1	Brooker 38
16 October	LDV Vans v Swansea (a)	2–1	Lehmann 45; Steele 89	1 March	Stoke (a)	1–3	Steele 54
20 October	Oldham (h)	3–0	Rogers 7; Steele 14, 28	5 March	Wycombe (h)	4–0	Zamora 40, 76; Brooker 58; Watson 81
23 October	Notts County (a)	2–2	Hart 63; Zamora 74				
27 October	Colchester (h)	1–0	Zamora 16	9 March	Reading (a)	0–0	
30 October	LDV Vans v Wycombe (h)	2–1	*(Albion win by golden goal)* Pitcher 45; Melton 92	12 March	Northampton (h)	2–0	Zamora 37; Morgan 59
				16 March	Bury (h)	2–1	OG 21; Zamora 45 (pen)
3 November	Bristol City (a)	1–0	Zamora 37	23 March	Notts County (h)	2–2	Zamora 5; Webb 48
10 November	Port Vale (h)	1–0	Zamora 49	30 March	Colchester (a)	4–1	Carpenter 23, 90; Gray 26; Brooker 29
17 November	FA Cup v Shrewsbury (h)	1–0	Zamora 31				
21 November	Peterborough (h)	1–1	Zamora 12 (pen)	1 April	Bristol City (h)	2–1	Lewis 40; Steele 90
24 November	Swindon (a)	1–1	Zamora 14	6 April	Peterborough (a)	1–0	Zamora 63
1 December	Bury (a)	2–0	Brooker 18; Zamora 60	13 April	Swindon (h)	0–0	
4 December	LDV Vans v Cambridge (a)	1–2	*(Albion lose by golden goal)* Melton 35	20 April	Port Vale (a)	1–0	Watson 72

Order your prints...

All the photographs featured in this book are available to buy in colour. You can get your prints by sending a written order stating:

- how many prints you would like
- the page no. on which the picture appears in the book
- what the picture shows
- the size/sizes you want for each print

to Bennett Dean, Flat 4, 18 St Michael's Place, Brighton BN1 3FT.

Please include a cheque for the full amount (see below).

Make cheques payable to **Pitch Publishing Ltd**.

Size	Price
9" x 6"	£5·00
10" x 8"	£7·00
12" x 8"	£7·50

Please add 50p for postage and packing.

Please allow 6 weeks for delivery.